new country KITCHENS

Country Living

new country
KITCHENS

TEXT BY

Rebecca Sawyer-Fay

FOREWORD BY

Rachel Newman

INTRODUCTION BY

Nancy Mernit Soriano

HEARST BOOKS
new york

Library of Congress Cataloging-in-Publication Data

Sawyer-Faye, Rebecca,
    Country living new country kitchens / text by Rebecca Sawyer-Faye :
foreword by Rachel Newman : introduction by Elizabeth V. Warren,
        p.   cm.
    Includes index.
    ISBN 0–688–12586–7
    1. Kitchens. I. Country living (Columbus, Ohio) II. Title.
    TX653.S25   1995
    643'.3—dc20   95–10885
                                                         CIP

PRINTED IN SINGAPORE

First Edition
1   2   3   4   5   6   7   8   9   10

Country Living STAFF

Rachel Newman, Editor-in-Chief • Niña Williams, Executive Editor • Julio Vega, Art Director
Mary R. Roby, Managing Editor • Nancy Mernit Soriano, Home Building and Architecture Editor
John Mack Carter, President, Hearst Magazine Enterprises

produced by SMALLWOOD & STEWART, INC., NEW YORK CITY

edited by RACHEL CARLEY • *designed by* SUSI OBERHELMAN • *illustrations by* ED LAM

CONTENTS

In the early days of *Country Living* magazine, we discovered that the first room in the house to "go country" was the kitchen. While we expected to encounter these welcoming rooms in classic country-style homes, we found them in formal homes, contemporary houses, and modern apartments as well. The breadth and variety of today's country kitchen led us to realize that our readers express their personalities

F O R E W O R D

most creatively in this one room — and that these expressions of creativity are limitless. No matter what the style of house, the country kitchen becomes a reflection of the homeowners' interests, a showplace for their collections, the palette for their color sense. And because the kitchen is traditionally the central gathering place for all family members, it echoes the sounds of family life.

The collection of country kitchens presented in this book spans centuries, continents, and lifestyles. They range in style from 18th-century primitive to contemporary Swedish, include pristine white rooms flooded with sunlight and dark-paneled hideaways warmed by crackling fires, and ably serve everyone from single professionals and young couples to large families. Despite their differences, however, all of these kitchens are infused with the sense of hospitality and comfort that defines the country way of life.

As a member of the *Country Living* family, chances are good that you may be about to build your first home or restore a period landmark. Or perhaps you have reached that stage when you are ready to remodel an outdated room to create your dream kitchen at last. Whatever your plans, we hope the kitchens in this book, filled with love, warmth, and good spirits, will inspire and encourage you. For every room there is a story, and we welcome the opportunity to share the stories with you.

RACHEL NEWMAN

Ever since the first kind cook asked a visitor to take a seat beside the hearth, country kitchens have been warming the soul as well as the body. Here is the true heart of the home, where friendly get-togethers and good conversation are as commonplace as the tempting aromas of home-cooked food. Indeed, hospitality is the very essence of country living: Even in more formal times, when it was fashionable to keep

INTRODUCTION

guests out of the kitchen, country cooks always left the door open, hoping for company while apples were peeled and pies baked.

That genial invitation to come in and stay awhile has never been more important, for these days everyone seems to be gathering in the kitchen. While this indispensable room continues to fulfill its traditional role as the cook's domain, it now also serves as dining room, living room, workroom, study, and even playroom in order to meet a broadening range of needs and lifestyles. This, in fact, is the *new* country kitchen: a comfortable, often multipurpose room where families are as likely to be found entertaining guests, watching television, or doing homework as they are preparing a meal.

Because the kitchen is now so clearly in the spotlight, we want it to look its best. More important, we want it to reflect our own individual tastes while drawing people of all generations together for food and fellowship. No style better satisfies this aim than country. As the extraordinary range of rooms presented in *Country Living New Country Kitchens* so dramatically demonstrates, homeowners across the nation are continuing to expand the definition of the country kitchen to accommodate state-of-the-art appliances, as well as comfortable, overstuffed furniture and even fine antiques. Here, they display collections and family heirlooms, incorporate craft traditions and folk art from other lands, and exhibit their own artwork and hand-craftsmanship. Clearly, these families are secure in the knowledge that hard and fast rules have no place in creating a great country kitchen.

As I have traveled around the country with other *Country Living* editors to photograph the kitchens, keeping rooms, and dining rooms that appear in our pages, I have noticed that the most successful rooms are almost always shaped by a homeowner's individual interests. Does he or she enjoy entertaining in the kitchen? Are the owners serious chefs? Does the family include small children? The answer to such questions are invariably reflected in the final design. We've also noticed that for every design dilemma, a solution exists. Whether the problem is a shortage of seating or storage, an inefficient layout, or an uninspiring decor, the sheer variety of possibilities offered by country style means a remedy can be found to suit any budget.

Fortunately, the selection of appliances, storage units and cabinetry, furniture, and surfacing materials has never been greater. Contemporary stoves, refrigerators, and other appliances are now available in a host of colors, finishes, designs, and models. Homeowners shopping for cabinetry may also be surprised to find an enormous range of ready-made stock styles. New easy-care finishes, such as resin-based solid surfacing, are continually introduced and improved as well.

Sometimes, however, the choices may be *too* great and can make the prospect of designing or remodeling a kitchen a daunting one. Luckily, help does exist. If you intend to make a major purchase, you can learn a lot on your own by visiting a kitchen design showroom. Here you can browse through catalogues and see cabinets, flooring, countertops, and appliances installed in actual room settings. A good salesperson should provide information regarding dimensions, energy usage, and prices. (Some showrooms even offer the services of their own staff designers.)

Don't be afraid to ask for professional advice. Among those who can provide valuable help are architects, interior designers, and certified kitchen designers. Architects can deal with structural problems and are particularly useful in laying out space, and an interior designer can help you with cosmetic and decorating decisions. A certified kitchen designer (C.K.D.) is trained to meet professional requirements in kitchen design and has a full understanding of standard measurements, wiring, plumbing, and building codes.

Such professionals can help you plan a budget and are also familiar with the full range of available design options, including appliances, cabinet styles, and countertop and flooring materials. It is often possible to find the right professional through word of mouth; the American Institute of Architects or the National Kitchen and Bath

Association (see Kitchen Resources, page 188) will also supply the names of designers in the region of the country where you live. Before making a decision, ask to see examples of finished work (photographs will usually suffice), and obtain references. Above all, be sure to meet the candidate face-to-face. Knowing that your styles "mesh" and that the right chemistry exists can be more important than obtaining the lowest possible cost estimate. Nothing will make up for the disappointment of a finished project that doesn't meet your expectations because you and your designer haven't been able to communicate. And always remember, the role of a professional architect or designer is to help *you*.

After choosing a designer or architect, bring as much material as possible to your first meeting. This might include fabric and color swatches, hardware samples (if you have something specific in mind), and photographs of kitchens clipped from magazines and brochures. Clearly state any special requirements, such as shelving for cookbooks or display areas for collections or artwork. Be prepared to describe in detail exactly how you would like to use your kitchen. Will serious cooking go on here? Will you be entertaining large groups? Do you have space requirements for projects? Even if you choose to tackle the job without the help of a professional, all these issues should be addressed before work begins.

One final point: You don't have to remodel a kitchen to make it your own. Many of the kitchens we show on these pages were created by homeowners without any professional help, and often without a single new purchase. Even a few well-chosen accessories — mementos of a trip, perhaps, or favorite flea-market finds — can transform a room with your personal imprint.

In the end, what matters most in a country kitchen is that it both function well and convey a sense of warmth, roles that have remained unchanged since the days when the farm family and hired hands gathered around the table to plan the day's work and feast on the hearty breakfast that would fuel their endeavors. Today, in our era of high technology and high stress, the solace offered by a well-designed country kitchen is as important as it ever was.

NANCY MERNIT SORIANO
Home Building and Architecture Editor

KITCHE

N s t y l e

WELCOME TO THE NEW
COUNTRY KITCHEN. ADAPTING WITH
EASE TO TODAY'S CHANGING
LIFESTYLES, THIS TRUE HEART OF
THE HOME NOT ONLY COMBINES
COMFORT WITH PRACTICALITY, BUT
ALSO REFLECTS A REMARKABLY
DIVERSE RANGE OF LOOKS AND TASTES,
FROM RURAL FARMHOUSE TO
CITY APARTMENT, WE INVITE YOU TO
SHARE SOME OF OUR FAVORITES.

Despite the availability of new materials and appliances, tradition still holds fast in the classic country kitchen. A fitting companion to the 1785 Vermont house it occupies, a newly designed interior (opposite) derives historic character from cabinetry and shelves made of salvaged wood. Recycled as a work island, the antique pine dry sink helped inspire the rustic decor. Original to the house, the nearby pine-paneled keeping room (above) still serves its customary role as an all-purpose room used for dining,

visiting, and staying warm by the fire. The careful restoration involved removing 200 years' worth of paper, paint, and plaster. The paneled door to the left of the fireplace conceals a bake oven. Both the plate rack, mounted over the deacon's bench, and the herb-drying rack are original to the structure.

A massive fireplace and oven dominate the kitchen outbuilding of an early Florida boardinghouse (overleaf). The whitewashed room is furnished much as it was in the late 1700s.

An urban kitchen can say
"country" as eloquently as a rural
one. In this New York City
apartment, plump cushions, lace-
trimmed breakfront shelves,
and curtains fashioned from an
antique organdy bedspread (left)
suggest a feminine hand at
work. Brass fittings and a white
ceramic-tile backsplash (above)
evoke Victorian times. Throughout
the room, pots of flowers and
aromatic herbs, including basil and
rosemary, offer a touch of nature
often missing in city kitchens.

In an 1869 Connecticut house, a Victorian-style light fixture hangs from a reproduction molded-tin ceiling to enhance the period look of the dining area (above). A custom-made maple base anchors the original sink (right), and glass-front cabinet doors — salvaged from an adjacent pantry — fit new custom-made cupboards. The copper range hood and Portuguese tiles lend European flair.

Introducing bold color is one
of the easiest ways to give a tired
kitchen a new lease on life.
Apple-red accents, modern track
lighting, and vintage dishware perk
up a simple but cheerful kitchen
(opposite) added onto a one-room
schoolhouse in the 1940s. Crisp
whites and a graphic checkerboard
floor pattern, in turn, rejuvenate
the remodeled kitchen of an 1892

North Carolina home (above).
The two antique painted step-
back cupboards set against the
wall are an innovative storage
alternative to the old metal
cabinets, which the owners
removed; the electric Hotpoint
stove and enamel-top table both
date from the 1920s.

 Black and white — a classic
color scheme with a timeless

appeal — proved an appropriate
choice for a kitchen decor with
traditional overtones (overleaf).
Remodeled from a former
butler's pantry and service
kitchen, the room features old-
fashioned glass-front cabinet
doors, period lighting fixtures,
and a hardwood floor. The
black marble countertops add a
note of contemporary drama.

As the heart of the home,
today's country kitchen often
incorporates eating and sitting
areas, ideal for family dining
and entertaining. Informal meals
take place in a traditionally
decorated room (opposite),
furnished with an 18th-century
settle table (the top folds up).
Distressed-wood cabinets and
a brick floor punctuate the rustic
country look.

In a multipurpose Vermont
kitchen, simple barstools turn an
island workstation into a handy
breakfast bar (above left). The
space flows into an adjacent
foyer and dining room, opened
up with a beamed cathedral
ceiling (above right).

Plump armchairs and a wicker
table define smaller living and
dining areas in a generously
proportioned kitchen (overleaf).

This sunny country kitchen
was inspired by a Swedish stuga,
or all-purpose room, a gathering
place where friends and family
can keep the cook company.
Situated by the French doors
(above), an upholstered sofa and
chairs offer an invitation to
sit and relax. A dining table is
conveniently placed next to
the open cooking area (opposite),
where a tile-topped peninsula
provides a serviceable work
surface. The beaded-board pine
cabinet and refrigerator panels
were deliberately designed
to complement the sitting-area
wainscoting. The decor of the
well-planned room owes its
vigor to a crisp Scandinavian
color scheme of cobalt blue and
soft naturals. Striking accents
include the hanging light fixture,
made of buffed steel.

Eye-catching ceiling treatments can bring interest and dimension to a kitchen decor. In this Colonial farmhouse kitchen, the original framing timbers were left exposed to preserve a rustic country spirit. A beam makes a handy storage place for pots and baskets (above), while pocket windows over the sink (left) allow the chef to converse with dinner guests in the adjacent dining room.

Formerly dark and cramped,
this Illinois kitchen received a
facelift from top to bottom,
starting with an application of
vine-printed wall covering on
the ceiling (above). Glass-front
cabinets suggest the look of
built-in hutches, which were
popular in the 1920s, when the
house was built. A butler's
pantry was reborn as the adjacent
breakfast room (right).

Natural wood can endow
any country kitchen with texture,
warmth, and a sense of history.
Hand-hewn posts and beams
were left intact in a 1790s farmhouse kitchen (above), remodeled
to incorporate additional
counter space and a small dining
area. Simple cupboard doors
with fielded (raised) paneling
recall Shaker woodworking.
A hand-painted portrait of the
farmhouse adorns the range hood.

In a new Colorado cabin
(opposite), pine logs chinked
with plaster lend pioneer
spirit. Instead of built-in wall
cabinets, the owners opted for a
Norwegian spice box and
an antique plate rack, which flank
the window. Beneath a simple
pine table that serves as a work
island, an immigrant's trunk
safeguards provisions of sugar
and flour. The swing was rigged
by a family member.

A welcoming space for dining is as important to country hospitality as a warm, friendly kitchen. The owners of a California cottage by the sea (opposite) use their dining room to display their own pottery and artwork. A remote Maine cabin is the setting for a snug eating area (above), filled with a collection of antique oil lamps and teapots. The furnishings of a sparely decorated dining room in a Los Angeles residence (right) reveal a strong conviction that less is more.

*Antiques are put to work daily
in the dining area of this
1745 log house. Stenciled chairs,
which were crafted by a local
furniture maker in 1881, surround
a table set with flow-blue plates
(left). More blue-decorated china
fills an 1840 cupboard, notched
long ago to hold a collection of
heirloom spoons (above).*

*In the dining nook of an 1940s
farm cottage (overleaf), windows
open outward, boat fashion, to
take in the Long Island landscape.*

The owners of this 1855
Canadian farmhouse (the farm
has been in the same family
since 1784) still take meals in
the original kitchen. The double-
decker wood-burning cook
stove (above) comes in handy
for simmering stews and soups —
and helps to heat the entire
house. A circa-1800 step-back
cupboard displays a fine collection
of flow-blue china (right); the
harvest table is made of pine.

KITCHEN

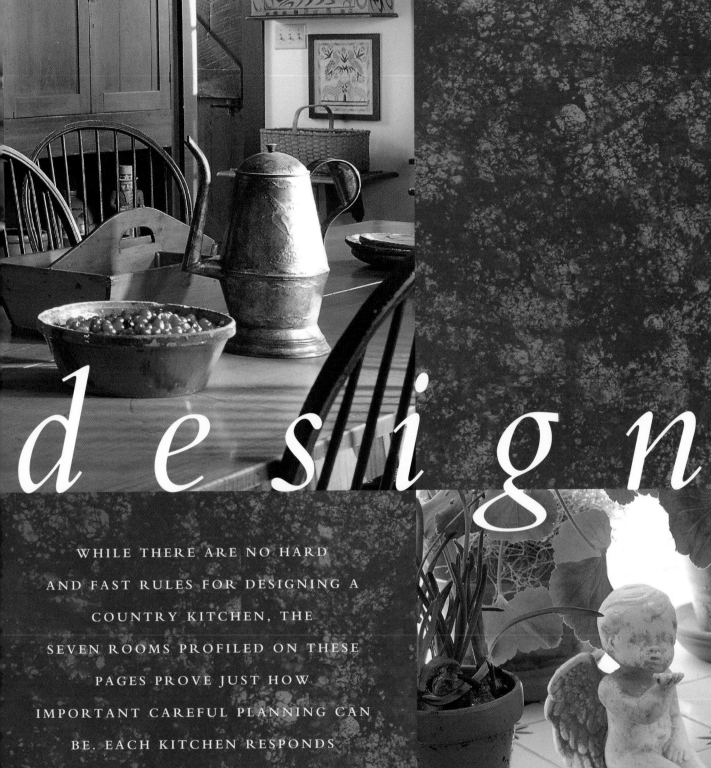

designs

WHILE THERE ARE NO HARD
AND FAST RULES FOR DESIGNING A
COUNTRY KITCHEN, THE
SEVEN ROOMS PROFILED ON THESE
PAGES PROVE JUST HOW
IMPORTANT CAREFUL PLANNING CAN
BE. EACH KITCHEN RESPONDS
TO DIFFERENT TASTES, NEEDS, AND
BUDGETS, BUT ALL REFLECT
THE PERSONAL STYLE THAT IS THE
VERY ESSENCE OF "COUNTRY."

With its warm wood tones, handcrafted detail, and intimate atmosphere, this classic country keeping room clearly dates back to another century. Or does it? In reality, the traditionally styled room and sunny adjoining kitchen are located in an Ohio house built just two decades ago on family land by David Smith, a craftsman highly regarded for his historically accurate reproductions of Early American

TRADITIONAL

furnishings. Frustrated by the high prices of the antiques he admired, David decided to try his own hand at woodworking, teaching himself the old-fashioned way — by taking apart and rebuilding furniture he found at flea markets. The artisan then honed his skills by restoring heirloom tables and chairs, and in the process learned how to replicate a range of furniture styles, from Pilgrim to Empire. His fine renditions of 18th- and 19th-century American tables, Windsor chairs, folk art, and wrought-iron hardware produced by his family-run company, The Workshops of David T. Smith, have won acclaim from discriminating collectors across the country.

In a cozy keeping room (opposite), a generous fireplace is used for everything from baking bread to roasting chestnuts. The owners follow the traditional open-hearth method, lighting several small fires of different intensities to cook a variety of foods at the same time. Inspired by Ohio's pioneer past, the warm-spirited decor accommodates antiques and reproductions alike. The mantel showcases early-1800s Stahl pottery from Pennsylvania; the bow-back Windsor chairs were made by the owner's company, The Workshops of David T. Smith of Morrow, Ohio.

David's patiently acquired skills and a deep respect for American history are strikingly apparent in the rooms shown here. As in many pioneer homes, the keeping room is the true heart of the house, serving as living room, dining room, and gathering place in one. Used to hold heavy cookware, an iron crane suspended inside the five-foot-high fireplace that dominates the space was once used by the craftsman's grandmother. It still sees regular service, especially on Thanksgiving, when the family feast is prepared over the open hearth.

In the separate kitchen, David and his wife, Lora, established a comfortable, time-worn look by crafting wainscoting from weathered wood panels rescued from the attic of an old Shaker meetinghouse slated for demolition. The maple cupboards wear a grain-painted finish similar to the type used generations ago by itinerant artists to imitate expensive woods. For a lustrous two-toned effect, the cabinets were stained a base color of dark "Indian" red. A wad of window-glazing putty dipped in black enamel was then rolled on top to create the

grained design, which was sealed with varnish. Curly cherry — the same high-quality wood reserved for David's most demanding furniture projects — forms the countertops. Countless knife nicks and scratches add character to the counter surfaces by offering a permanent record of meals long past; an occasional treatment with mineral oil yields a rich, protective sheen. The deep overhangs at the ends double as small tables, served by David's handcrafted tavern stools, used as comfortable perches for family members to enjoy breakfast, do homework, or simply watch the cook at work.

In both rooms, attention to detail has enhanced the spirit of the American past that is so important to the family. Salt-glazed pottery, once used for storing foodstuffs, along with redware plates and mugs and handsome wrought-iron hardware, is an integral part of the decor. Conveniently on hand when it came time to add the finishing touches, all of these furnishings are reproductions from the Workshops' on-site kiln and forge. For the owners, they not only look right, but also provide an essential link to the past.

Three years in the making, the kitchen (left) is entirely hand-crafted. Except for the antique baskets hanging from the beams, nearly everything else is new-to-look-old, including the salt-glazed crocks and an Amish-style rug. (The floor tiles underneath were cut in quarters and laid on the diagonal to fit the compact space.) A reproduction wood-and-tin chandelier supplements light from the north-facing window. Modeled after a step-back cupboard in the Philadelphia Museum of Art, the generously proportioned keeping room hutch (opposite) was crafted and painted by the Workshops in the bright colors typical of early Pennsylvania German pieces. New redware lines the open shelves, while animal carvings — some by the owners' son — parade across the top.

Not all country kitchens derive their warmth from woodstoves and their charm from rustic furnishings. Inspired by the jewel-like tones and earthy textures of the American Southwest, the distinctive room shown here, for example, is a model of modern efficiency, where state-of-the-art equipment, ample storage space, and a well-conceived floor plan meet the needs of the most serious cook. The design, by

SOUTH *western*

Country Living editor Nancy Mernit Soriano and kitchen designer Alessandro De Gregori, deliberately incorporates such easy-care synthetic materials as laminate and solid surfacing finishes along with sleek stainless steel. Yet a careful blend of familiar country-style features, including sponged and checkerboard patterns, ample wood trim, and natural clay floor tiles, softens the contemporary edge and sends a message of well-being.

To "wake up" the space without overwhelming it, the designers chose a classic Santa Fe palette of russet and peacock: the colors of earth and sky. These rich hues mingle on a checkerboard backsplash and on panels applied to cabinets, drawer faces, and the refrigerator — all custom-cut from sponge-patterned laminate. More custom touches include the brushed-pewter cabinet and drawer knobs, which recall Native American jewelry designs, and a herringbone-patterned door reminiscent of those on adobe buildings in Arizona and New Mexico. Laid in stock-size eight-inch squares, the quarry-tile floor enhances the Southwestern look with its texture and warm earth tones.

Clearly the focal point of the room, the professional-quality stainless-steel cooktop and range hood feature a built-in grill and plate warmer in addition to four gas burners. The designers stress that stainless steel is no longer considered appropriate only for restaurant kitchens; in this room, they chose it for its cool, clean appearance and the contrast it provides to the natural wood and tile.

"Successful kitchens are about balance," explains Alessandro De Gregori. "You need cool and warm, soft and hard, light and dark." This room has them all.

A herringbone-patterned door and quarry-tile floor in warm earth tones embody the Southwestern country style in the entryway of this new country kitchen (opposite). The theme is strengthened by the smallest details, including the fluted silver-toned knobs on the built-in corner desk.

The overall kitchen design (overleaf) combines the cool look of stainless-steel appliances with warm wood accents. Recessed ceiling fixtures adequately light the 240-square-foot space. Lowered from the ceiling, cupboard tops provide extra storage space.

The professional-quality cooktop
with a stainless-steel hood
(opposite) is modeled on a
commercial appliance design but
intended for home use. Framed
with solid cherry, the custom-cut
drawer and cupboard panels
are removable and can be replaced
for a totally different look.
A checkerboard backsplash made
from squares of sponged-look
washable laminate (top right)
complements countertops
of peacock-blue solid surfacing
material, patterned to resemble
stone. Molded edges make
the sink basins (bottom right),
also fabricated of solid
surfacing material, especially
easy to clean; a periodic light
sanding removes scratches.
The appliance garage located to
the right of the sinks features
a louvered roll-top door.

The cool, fresh appearance of this Illinois country kitchen — a traditional design with a contemporary accent — belies the many facelifts the room has gone through over the years. The current owner remembers them all. As a teenager, she moved with her family to the 1916 Georgian Colonial house with her family and except for a hiatus at college has lived here ever since. It seemed that no matter how many

NEW *expressions*

coats of paint went onto the walls, the room still felt small, cold, and dark. Designed in an era when servants did the cooking and entertaining always took place in the formal living and dining rooms, the kitchen and adjoining butler's pantry were functional, but virtually devoid of character or charm.

While it has contemporary flair, this remodeled kitchen in a 1916 Illinois house remains country at heart, featuring familiar checkerboard motifs and a fresh decor dominated by teal blue — a "color with style," the owner says. A "trellised" wall made of lattice strips nailed and glued over plywood dominates the work area (opposite), where a wall oven and microwave now fill a space formerly occupied by an obsolete servants' staircase. Nestled in its own niche, the four-burner gas cooktop rests on built-in cupboards and drawers to keep cookware close at hand. Glazed ceramic tiles pave the niche and countertop (right), promising easy cleanup.

An old farm table refitted with casters and topped with granite-patterned solid surfacing material (opposite) travels around the kitchen, furnishing additional counter space at a moment's notice. On the sink side of the work area, the traditional paneled cabinetry with simple knobs is painted an elegant white, a counterpoint to the gray and teal blue in the color scheme. The window over the sink (right) is one of the room's few original features. A lace-trimmed curtain stitched from a vintage tablecloth adds a softening touch over the practical pleated shade below it. Raised from the bottom up, the shade lets in plenty of morning sunshine while preserving privacy.

The new design, the result of a five-month remodeling project in 1991, remains old-fashioned in character, featuring country-spirited checkerboard patterns in the floor and backsplash tile work. Yet the space is also blessed with the latest time-saving appliances, which not only contribute to a whole new look, but also make the eat-in kitchen and adjoining garden room relevant to today's more casual lifestyle.

After gutting the rear portion of the house, architect Stephen Knutson of Evanston, Illinois, lengthened the old kitchen by six feet to create a light-filled work area. Several existing features, including the butler's pantry and a servants' staircase (used in more recent years to store canned goods) were altered or removed. The focal point of the revamped work space is the unusual "trellised" wall — made with inexpensive preprimed plywood and lattice strips — designed to remind the owner of her garden even on the coldest winter days.

Painted teal blue, the latticed wall plays off the floor pattern, which boasts a grid of simple, standard two-inch-square ceramic tiles in gray and white with black accents. This bold flooring is continued into the spacious garden room, which is located in a new skylit breezeway designed to connect the house to the garage — making the trip from car to kitchen more pleasant during harsh Chicago winters.

A specially designed supplemental radiant-heating system installed beneath the ceramic-tile floor (here and in the kitchen area) also helps dispel winter's chill. Regulated with a separate thermostat, the new system heats only the floor, an area that is typically difficult to warm because hot air rises. The hardworking garden room is well suited to the removal of coats and boots. Complete with its own sink, this multipurpose space is ideal for potting plants, and entertaining, as well: Plenty of cabinets offer ample storage space for vases, pots, garden tools — and extra beverages for last-minute guests.

In the garden room, a skylight (left) allows potted herbs (which summer on outdoor patios) to survive frigid Illinois winters. The French doors lead to the living room. Cupboards distinguished by a cherry finish (opposite) surround the sink, while the easy-care countertop made of solid surfacing material and the water-resistant tile floor make this a practical place for potting plants. The floor grid echoes the graphic patterns of antique game boards on display, including a 1920 pachisi board hung on the diagonal. Floor-to-ceiling windows combine with the skylight to bring in plenty of natural sunlight.

Embracing a remarkably diverse design heritage, American country style owes much to the rich immigrant culture that shaped this nation; indeed, many of the furnishings, materials, architectural elements, and accessories sought after today have their origins in foreign lands. So when the time came to remodel the kitchen of her 35-year-old Connecticut home, it was only natural for designer

E U R O P E A N *f l a i r*

Jennifer Bret Fagan to borrow from a broad range of European traditions. While the sunny work area and adjacent sitting room have strong Scandinavian overtones, a number of Mediterranean-inspired accents — notably in the counter tiles, copperware, and printed fabrics — also introduce color and texture to the design.

The most unusual and striking feature of the new room is the magnificent Scandinavian stove (overleaf). Substituting for the open fireplace more typically seen in America, this wood-burning stove — with raised hearth, firebox, and chimney all sheathed in gleaming ceramic tiles — is clearly the focal point of both the sitting area (where comfortable seating offers an invitation to pull up close) and the cooking area (in direct view of the cheerful fire).

Such stoves, a hallmark of Swedish domesticity, feature compact soapstone interiors that absorb heat and radiate it for hours. The small, intense wood fires burn quickly, yet need less fuel than required by other types of woodstoves. This remarkably efficient design originated in a region where long, harsh winters make effective heating imperative; however, the appeal of this type of stove, now available in this country, is universal.

Jennifer also adopted another traditional Scandinavian device for coping with dark winters: an airy color scheme of soft, clear hues and lots of white to reflect maximum natural light and make the most of short days. In this cheerful kitchen, blue accents picked up in the tiles and porcelain sink set off walls of pale yellow and cupboards and trim detailed in a pure, bright white. A liberal display of wood — for the painted cabinets and the beaded-board covering chosen for the work

A deft blend of European design traditions establishes the warmth and coziness of a traditional country kitchen in a Connecticut home (opposite). The small rag rug is typical of those seen in Scandinavian homes, while the rush-seated bistro chairs are French Provincial in style. The owner paid ten dollars a pound for her Turkish copper cookware.

A graceful arch springing from fluted pilasters (overleaf) opens up the main kitchen work space to the newly created sitting area. The centrally placed Swedish stove radiates heat all day from a single morning fire.

Natural sunlight and a 20-inch-deep tiled windowsill provide a hospitable setting for potted plants (opposite). A band of Portuguese tiles in a classical acanthus-leaf pattern accents the sapphire blue of the sink. In the work island, a shallow prep sink (above left) made of brass (kept bright with occasional polishing) is used for rinsing vegetables and fruit; filled with ice, it also makes a great wine cooler during parties. Spice bottles fit neatly into a drawer, and a simple book niche and built-in wine rack provide additional storage (above right).

island and sitting-area wainscoting — is also traditional to Scandinavia, where dense forests offer a plentiful supply of the material. The natural oak floor of hand-pegged random-width boards is bleached to a white finish that allows the grain to show through. Complementing the white cabinetry, the soft, translucent effect helps underscore the prevailing design theme: Lighter is better.

Against this backdrop, the counterpoints of color and texture added by Jennifer to bring interest and variety to the kitchen decor reflect their own range of European design elements. With its wide assortment of sizes and shapes, the collection of hammered copper pots and pans from Turkey lends particular dazzle. Jennifer opted for Turkish copper over its French counterpart both because it is less expensive and because she feels its dimpled surface looks more "antique." Traditional French Provincial fabrics, known for their clear, saturated colors and bright, repetitive prints, were used to upholster the comfortable sitting-area furnishings, while the countertop and backsplash tiles were made in Portugal.

W hen Beverly McGuire left New York City for California's Hollywood Hills a few years ago, she vowed she would never have another sophisticated, monochrome kitchen. After arriving on the West Coast, she and co-designer Larry Schnur purchased a 1926 Spanish-style bungalow under the "H" in the HOLLYWOOD sign and set about remodeling the house from top to bottom. The couple

NOSTALGIA *time*

A taste for collecting exemplifies the country spirit in a California kitchen, where an eclectic counter-top display (opposite) shows off wooden utensils — both old and new — casually stored in a bucket and pitcher. There are also French bistro glasses and soap from a Parisian grocery; the green Depression-era glass once belonged to the owner's grandmother.

New windows helped open up the 230-square-foot space (overleaf), where white woodwork provides a fresh backdrop for a decor accented with bold splashes of color. The stool covers, emblazoned with tropical hibiscus blooms, are made from a 1940s curtain panel. Over the sink, a bamboo pole bought for five dollars at a local lumberyard makes a handy rod for curtains recycled from a vintage tablecloth.

made it a priority to create a sunny, efficient kitchen to replace the original cooking area, which was dark and cramped. The result is a bright, lighthearted room, whose tropical mood springs from Beverly's childhood memories of summers spent in Hawaii. The color scheme of white and aqua — Beverly calls them "happy swimming-pool colors" — provides a cheerful, unifying backdrop for the owners' impressive collections of dinnerware and textiles dating from the 1930s to the 1950s. Larry, who grew up in a formal house, says the kitchen makes him feel "like tap-dancing and playing the banjo."

The transformation of the space was so complete that by the time the work was done, the only original feature remaining was the door between the dining room and the kitchen. To save money, the pair did all of the planning and much of the construction themselves, visiting showrooms, comparing prices, and purchasing stock materials rather than opting for more expensive custom designs. Straight off the assembly line, the stock-size cabinets (a combination of glass-front and solid-paneled styles in a bright white finish) gained character from the simple addition of a crown molding, which is available by the foot at lumberyards. The cheerful floor covering was laid in a random pattern of inexpensive vinyl tiles in Beverly's favorite shades of peach, blue, and gray. For the countertops, the couple chose a nostalgic boomerang pattern (recently reintroduced) in aqua because it reminded them of their childhood in the 1950s.

Clearly at home in this free-spirited setting, the couple's collections of china, painted buckets, glassware, and utensils are liberally displayed on countertops, atop cupboards, and behind glass-front

doors, becoming the undisputed stars of the decor. On the prowl in California's famous flea markets, Beverly is naturally drawn to cups, saucers, trays, and even juice glasses decorated with palm trees and other exotic greenery that accent the room's tropical spirit. More great finds include vintage fabrics. Souvenir tea towels and tablecloths printed with maps of tourist destinations are a particular passion; Beverly and her friends enjoy guessing the vintages by looking to see which cities are missing from the map. A simple white curtain rod mounted on the island makes an great display rack for the collection, which includes towels from Guam and Cuba.

The couple is also drawn to bowls and pitchers made by such American manufactures as Bauer, Homer Laughlin (makers of the much-collected "Fiesta" dinnerware, introduced in 1939), as well as Hall, Roseville, and Haeger. To Beverly, however, color and shape are more important than the manufacturer. In particular, she covets anything in periwinkle blue and celadon green. And always she follows a strict rule: Never spend more than 60 dollars for a single item.

Plates and platters bearing tropical motifs perk up the wall behind the cooktop (above), fitted with a removable iron grill. Opposite, clockwise from top left: A streamlined faucet in a gooseneck design serves a single-basin sink; free of sink and cooktop, the work island doubles as a breakfast table; vintage china, including some Hall pitchers originally offered as premium giveaways, and stacks of linens make simple yet graphic displays that reveal an eye for color, pattern, and shape.

As in a European farmhouse of old, this intriguing kitchen has a warm, rustic character derived from thick plaster and fieldstone-like walls, floors of tile and oak, and a lustrous soapstone sink. Yet instead of taking in views of the rolling countryside, the combination cooking-dining-sitting area is actually located in a converted loft overlooking New York City's wholesale flower market. In 1908, when the former

URBAN *a f f a i r*

industrial building was constructed, the neighborhood was known as Tin Pan Alley and a printing press stood where the current owner, Kerry Fidler, now prepares and serves his meals.

Whimsical references to nature give this Manhattan apartment an appealing farmhouse spirit. A soapstone sink (opposite) was custom-made to fit the corner, as were cabinets of faux-bois patterned laminate, stacked above in cantilevered steps. Among the distinctive country touches are the cabinet knobs, fashioned from small river stones purchased at a garden supply store and drilled through the back.

Separate areas for cooking, eating, and sitting make the converted loft space ideal for one-room living (overleaf). Walls once blackened by ink from a turn-of-the-century printing press now cast a warm glow, thanks to five layers of peach-tinted plaster.

A designer with a fondness for natural materials — and those that suggest them — Kerry teamed up with colleague Greg Roach to shape a spirited, witty decor. Respecting the original fabric of the old building, the pair were careful to preserve the pressed-tin ceiling and hardwood floor. Then, mixing new (and often synthetic) materials in with the old, they transformed the empty space into an apartment where fantasy meets reality.

Here, half the fun is guessing what is real and what isn't. The cabinets, for example, appear to be wood, but are faced with faux-bois laminate (complemented by handles and knobs made from actual twigs and pebbles). Precast crushed stone was cleverly fashioned into a "fieldstone" facing for the island and sink backsplash, while the stone sink (real) fits snugly into a "granite" countertop (synthetic solid surfacing material); the same easy-care material in solid white is also used for countertops extending around the sitting area to form handy shelf space and deep windowsills. Even the chandelier has its roots in nature: The gnarled branchlike arms may be crafted from wrought-iron, but the design is pure whimsy.

Although the decor is playful, the room's layout is straightforward and efficient. A well-designed floor plan divides the 1,100-square-foot space into three distinct areas. A dropped ceiling with recessed lighting defines the marble-paved cooking area, where a work island equipped with a four-burner cooktop and generous counter space doubles as a

A rustic twig handle with bark intact (opposite top left) adds witty detail to a cabinet faced with "chickenwire" mesh. Flanked by built-in chopping blocks, the four-burner gas range (opposite top right) fits neatly into the work island. A periodic rubdown with mineral oil gives the soapstone sink (opposite bottom) added luster; the fabricated "fieldstone" backsplash looks as though it has been in place for years. Terra-cotta plates, hand-blown goblets, and a birch-bark basket add country accents to the dining table (above).

bar, allowing the cook to interact with guests. To one side of the island, a kilim rug demarcates the sitting area, and a table placed squarely in front of the sunny window creates a dining area; here, an upholstered bench also serves as a window seat. Tying the various zones together are walls of softest peach, created with five separate coats of plaster tinted with powdered pigments in ocher, pink, and yellow. The designers allowed each layer to dry, then scratched the surface with steel brushes and sandpaper to expose the previous coat and achieve a textured effect. To enhance its antique look, they also rubbed the old wood floor with white water-based paint, wiping it off while still damp to produce a soft sheen. Polyurethane protects the entire surface.

Throughout the room, custom-built cupboards lit from within display hand-blown glass, antique medicine bottles, and mismatched china to advantage. Additional farmhouse appeal comes from the earthy textures of baskets, textiles, and rustic furniture. Kerry, who is a serious cook, says the room is both a joy to work in and an inspiration for preparing the country Italian fare he and his friends prefer.

Pleasing yet practical design has long been a hallmark of the Shakers, a religious sect that was founded in England in 1747 and peaked in America during the mid-1800s. Now known the world over for their exquisitely crafted furniture and labor-saving inventions, these enterprising people believed that their work could always be improved; beauty was a natural result of practical designs. It is just

SIMPLY *shaker*

The United Society of Believers in Christ's Second Appearing — better known as the Shakers — are well known for their simple, elegant craftsmanship, clearly the inspiration for this model kitchen. Reminiscent of Shaker built-ins, custom-made cherry cupboards (opposite) feature a typically plain paneled design with simple knobs; a niche houses books and a microwave oven.

Supported by steel arms, a table for two pulls out from the center island and offers a place for cozy dinners at home (overleaf). Finishing touches include the familiar Shaker peg rail, once used to store everything from bonnets to chairs; mounted here under hanging cupboards, rows of pegs come in handy for hanging dried herbs, mugs, and utensils.

that timeless Shaker ethic of form following function that shaped this elegant kitchen, where efficient Shaker-based design proves well suited to today's cooking and entertaining needs.

Most notably, the composition, created by *Country Living* editor Nancy Mernit Soriano and certified kitchen designers Tim Aden and Mark Kreuger, draws on the precise, compact craftsmanship of Shaker cabinetry. Among the Shakers' best-known works are built-in cupboards and ingenious sewing desks with handy drawers and generously proportioned work surfaces. Inspired by Shaker antiques on display in museums, the designers recast the traditional sewing desk as a center island complete with cooktop and storage space. The double-decker work surface provides counter space for serving food as well as for cooking, while a pull-out table on one side seats two comfortably for informal meals and offers an additional work and serving area. Providing more storage, two tiers of cherry cupboards and stacked drawers with plain wood knobs line the walls.

Throughout the space, rich earth tones also honor the Shaker preference for mellow hues; black accents provided by the sink, appliances, and backsplash tiles in turn supply contemporary drama. The oak floor, cabinetry stained butternut gold with deep red trim, and a refrigerator fitted with specially designed wood panels lend Shaker-style grace, while the upper walls and ceiling, painted a warm maize color, help to unify the uncluttered space. Even the straight ladder-back chairs with woven tape seats in green and black — molded after classic Shaker pieces — reflect the simple, honest workmanship that is the lasting legacy of all Shaker design.

A countertop of hunter-green solid surfacing material with the look and feel of real stone surrounds a deep porcelain sink in basic black (above); the chrome faucet and soap dish are new, but have a nostalgic design. Fitted neatly into the center island, the four-burner gas cooktop (left) features a built-in grill. Down-draft vents eliminate the need for a range hood, keeping the look as spare as possible.

An alphabet board used by
Shakers to educate youngsters
inspired a graphic frieze (right),
fashioned with letters cut
from thin sheets of vinyl. A
built-in plate rack for everyday
dishes is mounted over a
stainless-steel prep sink; to the
right is a glass-front wine
cooler. When not in use, the
ingenious pull-out table tucks
back into the center work
island, much like a drawer.

KITCHEN

elements

CABINETS, STORAGE, FLOORING, WORK SURFACES, AND APPLIANCES ARE THE FOUNDATION OF ANY WELL-DESIGNED KITCHEN. CHOOSING THESE BASIC ELEMENTS WISELY MEANS CONSIDERING COST, EASE OF MAINTENANCE, AND DURABILITY — AS WELL AS COLOR AND PATTERN. HERE ARE SOME OF THE MOST POPULAR OPTIONS AVAILABLE TODAY.

The foundation of today's kitchen, built-in cabinets are a surprisingly recent innovation. Not until the 1930s did they replace the freestanding cupboards and dish dressers once used to store everything from china to cookware, but even then few homeowners could afford the new units, which had to be custom-made. By the close of World War II, however, America's newfound prosperity created a

KITCHEN*cabinets*

Glass-front cabinet doors show off collections of vintage ceramics, glassware, and utensils to advantage yet keep kitchenware free of dust. To highlight the 150-year-old beaded-board woodwork of the original spruce ceiling, the owners of a Maine farmhouse had their cabinets built to match (opposite). Single glass panes front the upper row of cupboards, where brass latches lend a shipshape look. Providing additional storage, an antique pine dresser with carved handles holds linens and flatware, while the large mason jars on top preserve colorful grains, candy, and dried fruit.

demand for manufactured cabinets, which were soon available in standard sizes at reasonable prices.

In recent times, a new focus on kitchen design has produced stock cabinets in a variety of styles that would astound homeowners of even 30 years ago. These ready-made cabinets are typically less expensive than custom-made woodwork because they are delivered straight from the factory in predetermined sizes. (Filler strips that close the gaps when ready-made cabinets don't fit an existing space exactly can also be purchased.) An enormous selection of interchangeable units, including the basic cabinets and special storage racks, such as those for wine, trays, and plates, is available. In addition, the many interior options — spice drawers, pull-out baskets, and lazy Susans — as well as dozens of materials, finishes, and hardware styles now enable you to shop for ready-made cabinets and still put together a personalized design suited to your own tastes and budget.

Among the most popular cabinet materials is wood, both hard (including maple, walnut, oak, beech, birch, and cherry) and soft (such as white pine and spruce). Stock wood cabinets are available preprimed and in numerous finishes, including varnish, color-tinted stains, and paint, and come in a variety of styles — plain, paneled, and glass-front, for example. Cooks who like the look of glass doors but prefer to conceal the clutter that lies behind them may opt for cabinets with beveled or frosted glass. Other materials, such as laminate and even stainless steel and painted metal, can also be found to harmonize with a range of country decors.

To create a customized look for new stock units (or to rejuvenate existing cabinetry), many homeowners trim them with inexpensive stock molding; vintage pulls, latches, and other hardware unearthed at flea markets and antiques shows also add character. Cabinets purchased unfinished in preprimed pine (less expensive than hardwoods) also take well to any number of painted finishes, ranging from simple staining and sealing to stippling, graining, pickling, and stenciling. Paper or vinyl wall covering is another possibility for personalizing factory-made units.

While stock cabinetry offers good flexibility, you may still want to have custom work done if you need units to fit unusual dimensions, have special storage requirements, or simply can't find satisfactory

Installed in 1910, glass-front cabinets lined with shirred curtains (above) are combined with paneled cupboards and built-in countertops. Multipaned glass-front cabinets hung from the ceiling separate a remodeled kitchen from the pantry (opposite). Crown moldings and brass hardware help the new cherry units harmonize with vintage woodwork throughout the house.

Imagination reigns in a kitchen fitted with cabinets made of recycled weathered pine boards (opposite); the glass doors once served as windows in an old barn. Painted with freehand designs over a solid-color base coat, glass-front cabinets become a vehicle for self-expression in a whimsical guest cottage (above). Curtains stitched from fruit-studded fabric line the cupboard doors and camouflage under-counter storage space.

colors, materials, or finishes in ready-made cupboards. Custom cabinetry — which may be made of barn siding, beaded boards, or paneling salvaged from old buildings — can still be reasonably priced.

All kitchen cabinetry, whether stock or custom-designed, will stand up to years of hard wear if it is well made. Always check to make sure that the joints are neat and tight, corners are plumb, doors hang evenly, and drawers slide smoothly. Doors and drawers should also withstand stress — children have been known to use lower drawers as stepstools — and finishes should be stain-resistant.

If you are hiring a carpenter to do custom work, be sure to get references. When shopping for stock cabinets, look for those manufactured by members of the National Kitchen Cabinet Association, who must meet a rigid code of standards designed to ensure that your new kitchen is as safe as it is attractive.

For those who prefer to conceal cupboard contents behind solid doors, imaginative treatments also abound. Oversized moldings in sawtooth and scallop profiles transform simple paneled cabinets handcrafted from poplar and birch (above). Finger paintings by the owners' children inspired the lighthearted painted decoration.

Opposite, clockwise from top left: Other treatments include a washable wall covering; stenciled folk-art motifs adapted from the painted decoration on a Pennsylvania German trunk; a graphic scheme of contrasting paint in bright solid colors; and punched-tin panels like those seen on early pie safes.

Quintessentially "country" are beaded-board cupboards — treated to a fresh coat of white paint but otherwise left untouched — in a 1940s farm cottage (overleaf). While they are actually built in, these cabinets have the look of freestanding storage pieces typical of traditional Early American kitchens.

PRETTY*trims*

Using simple trimmings to dress up shelves and cupboard doors is an inexpensive way to bring country character to any kitchen. Such detailing softens hard edges and provides welcome visual interest to otherwise utilitarian storage areas, suggesting the well-kept look of an old-fashioned linen closet.

Easily mounted on standard-size rods, curtains hung on the inside of glass cupboard doors, for example, will cleverly disguise clutter while lending a room additional color, texture, or pattern. Consider a fabric that coordinates with existing window treatments in your kitchen, or try ready-made translucent "sheers" for a soft, traditional look. Romantic lace panels attached inside the door with self-adhesive tape allow china and glassware to peek through without sacrificing a neat appearance.

Vintage linens, which can be picked up inexpensively at flea markets or tag sales, may also be put to use with great

effect. Try draping your shelves with tea towels, or lining up napkins folded into triangles and turned so the center points hang over the shelf edge. Lace doilies and antimacassars, as well as heirloom handkerchiefs, can also be arranged in this fashion — all with charming results.

Lace edging also works well for sprucing up pantry or kitchen shelves, while other sewing notions, such as broad ribbons and the richly embroidered upholstery tape used by professional drapers, can be transformed into eye-catching finishing touches. (Sold by the yard, dressmaking trims are found in fabric shops and some department stores.)

Paper shelf trims include wallpaper borders, which are available by the yard at home decorating centers, as well as shelf paper, sold in hardware stores. (Antique shops are a source for vintage paper borders.) Newspaper strips, fan-folded and cut into designs paper-doll fashion — recalling the traditional Pennsylvania German craft of scissors-cutting known as *Scherenschnitte* — are another idea. In short, there are no rules: The key is to experiment, and to have fun finding the trims you like.

Inventive storage is a hallmark of the country kitchen, where imaginative cooks not only make use of cabinets, racks, bins, and shelves, but also press into service a wide range of collectibles, such as unusual jars and old stoneware crocks. Baskets, buckets, and nostalgic-looking tins — grouped casually on a countertop, along a windowsill, or even on the floor — can come in handy for stashing utensils

R A C K S & *s t o r a g e*

and holding produce. A welcome addition to any kitchen, country furniture also provides much-needed extra space. In the end, the key is flexibility, for no matter how much kitchen storage is available, it is likely never to be enough.

While conventional wall cabinets are always a good option for keeping a room looking tidy, don't rule out open storage. Indeed, displaying cookware, utensils, and foodstuffs out in the open lends itself especially well to the warm and casual look associated with country kitchens; not everything must be tucked neatly out of sight. The traditional plate-drying rack, in particular, is a venerable means for storage and display of both heirloom and everyday dishes, while simple racks suspended from the ceiling or attached to a wall can handily hold everything from copper cookware to molds and graters. (Racks can be purchased new or made at home, perhaps from an old ladder or window frame.) Just as they did in America's early kitchens, utensils, pots, and baskets, as well as dried herbs, fruits, and Indian corn, might also hang from ceiling beams or Shaker-style peg rails. An inexpensive option, simple open shelving, in turn, is much favored by collectors eager to show off prized ceramics, pewter, and glassware.

In country kitchens, storage includes both the conventional and the unexpected. As decorative as it is functional, a plate rack keeps prized blue-and-white graniteware within easy reach (opposite). Creating a three-dimensional collage of shapes, copper pots hang from a beam. On the counter, a set of six storage cubbies rescued from a defunct railroad station now holds kitchen odds and ends. To the left of the dishwasher, a homespun curtain offers easy access to frequently used pots.

Among the country furnishings now used in the kitchen are commodious armoires, whose deep shelves prove as hospitable to table linens and stemware as they once did to clothing and bedding. Wall cupboards and dish dressers have migrated from dining rooms into less formal keeping rooms, and humble pie safes and jelly cupboards have left the pantry and regained their rightful place near the cook, helping to make the kitchen one of the friendliest rooms in the house.

Pewter plates gleam on a
drying rack mounted in front of
a sunny window (opposite),
while a collection of mid-19th-
century wireware holds pies, eggs,
and fruit. A contemporary pot
rack features ladderlike rungs
(above), while an old oxen yoke
from an antiques shop, fitted
with hooks, holds cookware at
a convenient height (right).

In a well-stocked country
kitchen (overleaf) cookware
literally climbs the walls on
simple wood racks outfitted with
standard metal "S" hooks.

Creative shelving serves a
U-shaped kitchen well in this
cheerful garage apartment.
Painted white, open shelves hold
pottery and foodstuffs, leaving
plenty of space for a pass-
through (opposite). A scallop-
edged drying rack fitted with
standard-size brass cup
hooks (above) allows glass to
sparkle and colorful pottery
to look its best.

Open storage is also the
rule in a country kitchen brim-
ming with cookware and
pottery (overleaf). Here simple
shelves were designed to showcase
an outstanding collection of blue-
and-white graniteware. Peg rails
and a vintage stove hold dishes,
cups, and crocks, and a step-back
cupboard is the perfect resting
place for plates and casually
stacked cups.

A good complement — or
alternative — to conventional
built-ins, freestanding cabinets
and one-of-a-kind cupboards
enjoy a place of honor in country
kitchens. Outstanding examples
include an unusual hand-painted
Norwegian wall cabinet (above);
a floor-to-ceiling wall unit
with drawers and paneled cupboards, rescued from a dismantled
farmhouse (opposite top); a
reproduction kitchen "safe" with
screened door (opposite bottom
left), and a primitive jelly
cupboard (opposite bottom right).

CARE OF *copper*

A superior heat conductor, copper has long been the metal of choice for kitchenware. Food not only heats quickly and cooks evenly in a copper pot or pan, but also cools rapidly when removed from the stovetop. Egg whites beaten in a copper bowl gain extra volume, owing to a complex chemical reaction that occurs when they touch the metal.

Since contact with copper can cause food to discolor and gives it a metallic taste, copper pots and pans are generally lined, often with a soft metal such as tin or nickel; newer cookware is sometimes finished with more durable stainless steel. (Avoid cooking in an unlined copper pot or pan.) To protect the lining when you cook, use wooden or plastic utensils.

Because copper tarnishes easily when exposed to food, liquids, and the air, it does require a little extra care if you want to keep it shiny. Mild detergent and a nylon sponge or natural-bristle brush are fine for day-to-day cleaning; avoid abrasive scouring compounds and steel wool, which can scratch the copper or wear through the lining. Bowls, the only copperware that is typically unlined, should be rinsed after cleaning with a solution of three parts water to one part vinegar; any residue of soap or grease will prevent egg whites from thickening.

A nonabrasive commercial metal polish will restore luster to copper cookware. You need not apply this after every washing, however, since a bit of verdigris (a greenish-blue deposit) only adds to the beauty of the metal and is not harmful in small amounts.

Be it a serviceable countertop, custom-designed island, or handy snack-bar peninsula, the best kitchen work area is both practical and good-looking. Choosing the right material for any work surface, however, can be confusing, since each has its own virtues and maintenance requirements; moreover, what works for one cook might not be suitable for another. Take the time to assess your budget, as well

WORK *surfaces*

as how a particular material might suit your cooking habits. You may want to try a mix of materials, adding a marble counter section for pastry preparation, for example, or a butcher-block insert for chopping. Cost of installation is another consideration.

One of the most popular choices for country kitchens is ceramic tile, which is available in both glazed (shiny) or matte (dull) finishes in an enormous variety of stock colors, patterns, and sizes (typically two to six inches square). Custom-designed tiles are also available and can be mixed in with stock as striking accents to keep costs down. Ceramic tiles are somewhat prone to chipping and do not provide a good cutting surface, but are heat-resistant and easy to clean.

A common choice is plastic laminate, which is marketed under a variety of brand names. Although it is not heatproof, laminate is often used for kitchen countertops because the selection of stock colors and patterns is so extensive and the material tends to be among the least expensive. A more durable (and more costly) alternative is a resin-based synthetic known as solid surfacing material, also sold by several manufacturers. As opposed to laminate, which is applied as a veneer, solid surfacing is molded to the countertop and can also be used to line sink basins. The extremely smooth material comes in neutrals and solid colors as well as faux marble and granite patterns that have the look of genuine stone without the tendency to discolor.

Real stone, of course, is also an option for country kitchens. The two most commonly used stone types for countertops are granite and marble, both of which can be purchased as tiles or as a continuous surface made from thin, machine-cut slabs. Granite is durable and

A ceramic-tile countertop and coordinating backsplash make a strong design statement while offering a heatproof, easy-to-clean work surface (opposite). The sponge-patterned tiles are accented by a border in a hand-painted fleur-de-lis pattern. For interest and contrast, the countertop tiles were laid on a diagonal. Because ceramic tiles can chip and crack, it's a good idea to keep spares on hand for future repairs.

Ceramic tile comes in a broad selection of shapes, patterns, and colors, including the shiny blue-glazed Mexican tiles used in a Santa Fe kitchen (above), white squares with a Delft-like pattern (left), and oblong glazed "bricks" (opposite). Tiles are best set closely together to minimize the grout lines, which should be sealed to keep out mildew and grime. Both white and colored grouts are available to match — or contrast — with the tiling.

heat-resistant, though it tends to stain. Marble, also prone to staining, offers a cool, smooth surface that is great for rolling out pastry dough. Slate is another popular countertop material, often used in sink areas because it is waterproof. Less porous than marble, it is especially hard-wearing. Soapstone is softer than marble, but is proven to be more resistant to acids, heat, and stains.

Traditionalists who favor natural materials will also want to consider aged hardwoods, such as maple and oak, which in time take on an antique, mellow appearance. Wood must be kept scrupulously clean, as it tends to absorb and retain oils and bacteria.

Manufactured in four-by-eight-foot sheets, resin-based solid surfacing material (above) can be contoured to fit different shapes and permits near-seamless surfaces. In contrast to laminate veneers, colors and patterns penetrate the entire depth of the material.

While a marble work surface is often favored by bakers, the smooth finish of solid surfacing is also good for pastry preparation. A built-in bake center made of the durable material (above) was installed a few inches below standard countertop height for easy rolling.

Work areas should be as generously sized as possible. In a small kitchen, a minimum of 2½ linear feet of counter space is recommended for food preparation, with an additional 2 feet next to the sink. Larger kitchens should include ample countertop by the stove and refrigerator. An island workstation will provide extra counter, storage, and dining space and permit a more flexible kitchen layout, as it can accommodate a sink and cooktop. A peninsula can also double as a dining area and makes an effective space divider in a large room. Even a small table or butcher block will make preparation and cleanup easier by providing a bit of extra work surface.

Thick slabs of polished
New York State slate make a
handsome countertop (above);
the dense stone is especially
hard-wearing. Natural striations
distinguish soapstone (left),
which is impervious to lemon
juice and other acids. A monthly
rubdown with mineral oil and
gentle sanding helps to remove
scratches and maintain a natural
luster. The speckled markings
of granite (opposite) give the
durable stone a look of depth
and texture. Bullnose edging is
a soft finishing touch.

A bi-level wood countertop
offers two convenient work levels
in a rustic country kitchen
(opposite); recycled floorboards
make an effective camouflage
for the clothes dryer. Varnished
for protection, salvaged wood
from a farm once belonging
to the owner's father creates a
handsome surface for the

countertop in a remodeled
kitchen (above). While wood
is prone to nicks and water
stains that accumulate over time,
these "blemishes" also give
a wood surface character. Rubbing
occasionally with mineral oil
(rinse with hot sudsy water
and dry thoroughly) will restore
its natural luster.

Providing extra counter area,
work islands can be customized
to suit a variety of spaces and
uses. Fitted with a cooktop
and grill, a squared version with
one corner lopped off provides
leg room for stools (opposite). An
elongated granite-topped island
incorporates gas burners, prep
sink, snack bar, and bookcase
(above), while a marble-surfaced
beauty with a paneled fruitwood
base features rounded overhangs
for seating (right); for parties, it
doubles as a buffet.

A well-designed peninsula
nearly doubles the counter space
of a remodeled kitchen (opposite),
transforming an L-shaped plan
into a U-shaped layout. The
counter overhang accommodates
stools. Anchored to a wall,
a table becomes an unusual
peninsula in a tight area (above),
providing both dining and
work space. With its fluted
column base and trompe l'oeil
painted top, it also serves as
a decorative focal point.

In a pinch, a simple table can double as a useful work surface. An inexpensive alternative to a custom-designed work island, an enamel-topped table from the 1940s makes a handy baking center (opposite). An heirloom chopping block that once stood in a butcher shop belonging to the owner's grandfather now serves a Maine kitchen (above). Mounted on casters, the weighty block rolls away when it's time to wash the floor. Fitted with legs, an old millstone makes an unusual table (right).

KITCHEN *planning*

Although the traditional role of the American woman had placed her firmly in the kitchen since Colonial days, the idea of planning the room for efficiency and convenience did not earn any serious attention until the Victorian era. In 1869, the importance of good kitchen design was put into words in the popular household management guide *American Woman's Home* by the influential home economists Catharine E. Beecher and Harriet Beecher Stowe. "In most large houses, the table furniture, the cooking materials and utensils, the sink, and the eating-room are at such distances apart," the sisters complained, "that half the time and strength is employed in walking back and forth to collect and return the articles used."

The Beechers understood then, as we do now, that the best appliances and work surfaces will not help a kitchen function well if the layout itself is not convenient. To save the cook steps and ensure plenty of elbow room, today's designers often rely on a planning device known as the work triangle. Developed through university studies in the 1950s, this standard formula for efficient traffic patterns is based on an imaginary triangle measured from sink to stove to refrigerator. The sink should be 4 to 6 feet from the stove and 4 to 7 feet from the refrigerator; a distance of

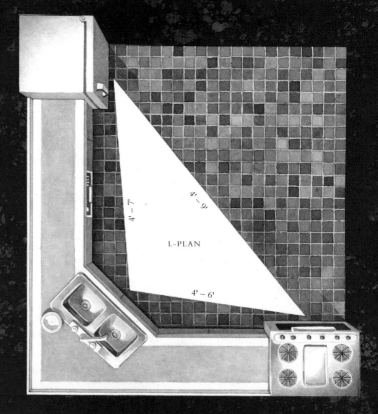

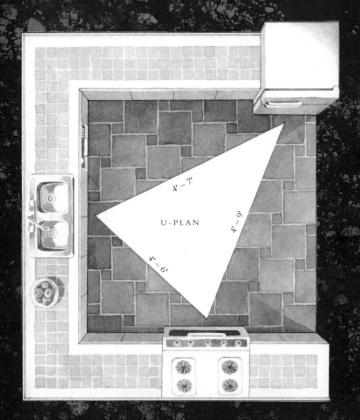

U-PLAN

4' – 7'
4' – 9'
4' – 6'

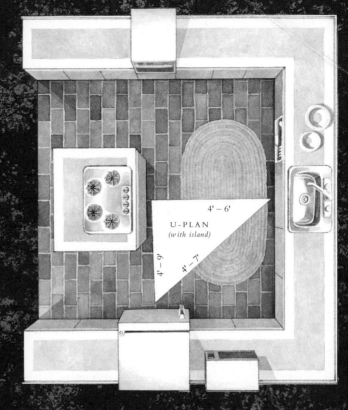

U-PLAN
(with island)

4' – 6'
4' – 9'
4' – 7'

4 to 9 feet is recommended between the stove and refrigerator. The sum of the three measurements (or sides of the triangle) should be at least 12 feet but not more than 22 feet. The diagrams shown here illustrate how this concept might apply in four typical kitchen layouts: the L-plan, the U-plan (with and without a work island), and the two-sided galley. The work triangle, however, is meant as a guideline, not a rule, and good kitchen layouts can have numerous variations. The final design always depends on the personal needs of the cook.

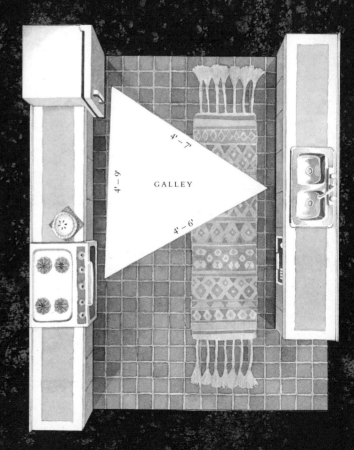

GALLEY

4' – 7'
4' – 9'
4' – 6'

Country flooring has come a long way since Colonial days, when a layer of sand swept into a decorative pattern atop a crude board floor was the mark of a fine housekeeper. In place of sand, once used to absorb spills and odors, today's cooks now tread on durable, easy-care flooring made of new synthetics as well as more traditional alternatives such as brick, stone, and wood. Most of the floor materials used today

STYLISH *floors*

fall into one of two basic categories: "resilient" (soft synthetics and wood) and "non-resilient" (stone and tile). Vinyl (actually polyvinyl chloride, or PVC) is the most commonly available resilient flooring. It comes in tiles as well as in sheets (in 6-, 9-, and 12-foot widths), which offer the advantage of a smooth surface with few soil-collecting seams. Fixed with an adhesive, vinyl can be removed more easily than ceramic tile, which is cemented down, so it is a good choice for homeowners who redecorate periodically. Moreover, vinyl recovers easily from indentations, absorbs sound, is comfortable underfoot, is relatively inexpensive, and offers a huge range of colors and patterns.

Antique bricks pave the floor in a Kentucky kitchen (opposite). Often found at demolition sites and salvage-supply centers, old bricks have a softer look than newly minted pavers and can be used to link a kitchen to an outdoor patio. Basketweave and herringbone patterns provide added interest. When choosing among the dozens of flooring options now available, consider durability, price, ease of care, installation cost, and appearance. A non-resilient floor covering such as brick, for example, tends to be hard underfoot and amplifies noise, but many homeowners feel its natural beauty more than compensates.

An especially handsome type of resilient flooring is wood flooring, which may be laid in wide planks, narrow boards (known as strip flooring), and parquet-style squares, called blocks. Choose among handsome hardwoods such as oak, maple, beech, birch, and hickory, and less expensive softwoods, such as Southern yellow pine and Douglas fir, which are well suited to stenciling, prickling, or graining. For protection, wood floors should be treated with a penetrating sealer or a varnish such as polyurethane.

While "naturals" such as ceramic tile, brick, stone, and slate can be costly, these non-resilient floor coverings are also beautiful. For safety, ceramic tiles are generally sold in a matte, or non-glazed, finish rather than the more slippery glazed version used on countertops, but they still come in a vast array of stock colors and patterns. Earth-toned quarry tiles of porous clay (fired at lower temperatures than ceramic tiles) are another option. All clay tiles should be professionally installed over a stable subfloor to guard against chipping and breakage.

Tiles laid in contrasting
patterns can help divide a room
into distinct sections and provide
color and pattern. *Opposite,
clockwise from top left:* Victorian-
style hexagons join a field of
stock-size two-inch black squares
to visually separate kitchen
from pantry; solid-color squares
define an eating area; stock
tiles are used in a graphic checkerboard pattern; dark-colored
grout (made from finely powdered
cement) contrasts with white
tiles and helps camouflage soil.
In a city kitchen (*right*), hand-
made quarry tiles help create
the look of a European farmhouse;
the tiled wall mural dictated
the color scheme. Installing floor
tiles after cabinets and large
appliances are in place will save
you tiles — and money.

Although it is among the least costly floor-covering options on the market, vinyl doesn't have to be boring. Laid on the diagonal, stock vinyl tiles mimic the traditional checkerboard pattern that was so popular in Colonial times (opposite).

A diamond pattern is the focal point of a kitchen (above left), and wide stripes make a bold statement in a dining room (above right). These two floors, custom-cut from sheet vinyl, in the same country cabin, recall Amish quilt designs.

Painting underfoot is an American tradition dating back the 1700s, when milk paint was used to extend the life of soft pine floorboards. Bold patterns are still popular today. Imitating a woven carpet, a trompe l'oeil design applied with oil paints boasts a "tasseled" border (opposite). In a Long Island, New York, dining room, black-and-white checks supply classic country styling (above). Hand-painted over oak flooring, an intricate pattern with a central floral medallion provides drama underfoot (right).

FLOOR*cloths*

From as early as the 1600s to the mid-19th century, when linoleum was invented, housekeepers regularly relied on painted canvas floorcloths to protect wood floors from dirt, grease, and wear from heavy traffic. Used in kitchens, halls, and other areas where more costly floor coverings were impractical, the tough and washable cloths were also placed directly over rugs (typically under the dining room table) to keep them clean. Canvas floorcloths were designed both as area rugs and as wall-to-wall carpeting, which was tacked in place over a thin bedding of straw. The carpeting could easily be pried loose, rolled up, then taken outdoors to be shaken, scrubbed, and even repainted, if necessary.

Either imported from England or made locally, floorcloths were widely available in early America. While pro-

fessional "fancy" painters sold ready-made painted cloths (advertised in 1802 for about three dollars a square yard), many homemakers produced their own. Coated with a waterproofing oil, the canvas was stretched and sized, then allowed to cure prior to decoration. (One early-19th-century account tells of a Connecticut housewife who prepared her cloth by nailing it to the side of a barn.) At least three coats of paint and several protective layers of varnish followed, resulting in a floor covering that would see years of use.

Floorcloths, however, were not just practical. They were also, quite literally, the canvases on which both artists and homemakers honed their skills. Early cloths were typically of one color (yellow ocher was common), but all manner of patterns, both freehand and stenciled, were popular by the mid-1700s. Among these were geometrics and trompe l'oeil designs, often done with grain painting and marbling to imitate expensive wood and stone. The painted cloths did not only grace the floors of simple houses; stunning examples were also found in the grandest dwellings, including the White House, where Thomas Jefferson had at

least one such floor covering installed during his tenancy from 1801 to 1809.

Today, canvas floorcloths like those shown here remain a popular and practical addition to kitchens and dining rooms. The methods for making them have not changed much. Extra-heavy artist's cotton canvas is the recommended fabric; this should be sealed and waterproofed with a coat of oil-based paint. Water-soluble acrylics work well for painting on the design. Be sure to protect your artwork with several coats of varnish, which will guarantee years of wear.

Before electric refrigerators first came on the market around the time of World War I, keeping food cold meant placing a 100-pound block of ice in an insulated wooden icebox and remembering to empty the drip pan every day. Factory-made iceboxes were introduced around the 1830s, but were not widespread until about the 1860s. The standard model featured an outer casing of heavy-duty oak or ash and

REFRIGERATORS

a lining of porcelain, zinc, or galvanized tin; insulation varied from crumpled paper to felt, cork, and even charcoal. By mid-century, ice was made and sold commercially, but before the first mechanical icemaking machine was patented in 1834, most country folk harvested their own from a nearby pond or stream. Packed with insulating sawdust or straw in an icehouse or a deep hole, the cut blocks could stay frozen for months.

A far cry from the early models, today's electric refrigerators feature energy-efficient designs, temperature and humidity controls, automatic defrosting systems, and convenient options such as adjustable shelves and bins, cold-water dispensers, and automatic icemakers. Yet while the new refrigerator-freezers are a welcome addition to the kitchen, they also rank among the most ungainly of appliances. Bulk alone is a problem: Many models are literal monuments to modern technology, measuring at least 5 feet tall and often extending into the room a good 16 inches beyond the standard 2-foot depth of cabinets and counters.

Fortunately, a refrigerator can meet contemporary needs and still be compatible with a country interior. Antique iceboxes, for example, have become popular collectibles and can be adapted to electricity. Geared to changing tastes and decorating needs, new refrigerator-freezers, in turn, now come with a choice of finishes, such as stainless steel or wood, and also can be finished with custom panels designed to match your own cabinetry or wood trim. Many homeowners, however, still opt for the old standby: a plain white refrigerator, which goes with everything and is, quite simply, itself.

Converted to electricity, a vintage icebox made of varnished golden oak with solid brass hardware suits an old-fashioned country kitchen (opposite). The upper compartment of this 1880 model originally held a block of ice. (A card hung in the kitchen window notified the iceman of the desired size.) As air around the ice chilled, it filtered to the lower food cabinet, forcing the warmer air there to rise. Before these conveniences became widely available in the mid-19th century, housewives stored dairy products and other perishables in a cool pantry, usually located on the north side of the house.

To complement the room's
cabinetry, a contemporary
refrigerator-freezer was finished
with wood paneling (opposite).
A no-nonsense commercial unit
(above) features an easy-to-
clean cabinet of stainless steel;
its straightforward lines suit
the unpretentious spirit of a
simple country kitchen. Custom-
painted floral motifs soften
the modern look of a new side-
by-side model (right), detailed
with crown molding and date,
much like an antique wardrobe.

If the kitchen is the heart of the home, the stove is what makes that heart beat. Be it an antique or modern adaptation, the right stove will bring warmth and coziness to any kitchen, providing a focal point and, often, a welcome connection to the past.

Of all the stoves ever produced, perhaps none evokes yesterday's country kitchens better than wood-burning models. Introduced in the

COUNTRY *stoves*

1830s (along with their counterparts fueled by coal) and used into this century, these cast-iron beauties take us back to a time when food was always home-cooked and fresh and enticing aromas permeated the house. The design is basic: Both vintage and reproduction versions typically include a firebox, where the fuel is burned, a stovepipe, an oven (more elaborate units have a second warming oven), and a good-sized cooking surface. Temperature of the stovetop is controlled not by a knob that raises or lowers a flame but rather by moving the pot from hotter to cooler parts of the cooking surface — the entire stovetop is thus used.

While wood-burning stoves can produce delicious meals, using one requires expertise and vigilance, both for even cooking and for safe operation. Consequently, many people who own one have a second, modern stove on hand. Those who prefer a vintage look but easy operation might opt for a reproduction cast-iron model actually fueled by gas or electricity, or a gas or electric model from the 1930s or 1940s. It is also possible to convert an old stove from one cooking fuel to another: wood-burning to gas, for example, or gas to electricity.

Preferred by many serious cooks, professional gas ranges are also finding their way into country kitchens. Since commercial stoves can be bulky and tend to give off a lot of heat, manufacturers are now producing professional ranges that have been specifically modified for home use. These eliminate the drawbacks without sacrificing the advantages — notably, extra-sturdy construction, a large number of burners (as many as eight), and special grill and griddle options. Smaller four-burner models are available for tight spaces as well.

Because of their good looks and good performance, wood-burning cookstoves have a particularly welcome place in today's country kitchen. This cast-iron Monarch with two warming drawers in the hood is still used daily to cook breakfast (opposite). The owner considers the stove, which once belonged to his grandmother, just as much an heirloom as the family china and silver. About three cords of wood will keep a wood-burning stove stoked for the winter; twice as much should be on hand if the stove is to be used all year. Some antique models are unearthed in the houses they originally served; others may be found at estate auctions or bought from dealers who specialize in old stoves.

Those who use cast-iron cookstoves swear by their ability to seal in natural flavors and moisture. Introduced in the 1930s, one popular commercial type is the English Aga cooker (top left); the burner covers invert to become warming trays. Reconditioned stoves are also well suited to country kitchens. A white-enameled 1930s gas range manufactured by O'Keefe & Merritt (bottom left) features two ovens and a warming tray. A 1929 General Electric Hotpoint stove occupies its own fireplace-like niche (opposite). With new wiring, this four-burner model is once again in active service. As graceful as it is functional, the stove has cabriole legs similar to those on Queen Anne furniture.

While it looks antique, a modern stove (overleaf) features electric burners; a firebox also accommodates coal or wood.

KEEPING *rooms*

Perhaps no place in the house embodies the hospitable spirit of "country" better than the keeping room, an informal room traditionally used for everything from sleeping to cooking over the open hearth. This adaptable space has its roots in the 17th-century Colonial "hall," a multipurpose room that, heated by a great walk-in fireplace, often served as a kitchen. Here, too, the children learned their lessons and the family engaged in daily Bible readings.

It is unclear when the particular term *keeping room* first came into use (in the 18th century, it actually referred to a formal parlor). Today, however, it is universally used to describe a large, comfortable gathering space, warmed in winter by a woodstove or blazing fire. The keeping room sometimes does double duty as a dining room, often furnished with well-worn Windsor chairs and a farm table. What better place to enjoy a leisurely hearthside meal?

Thanks to the wide variety of colors, styles, and materials available, modern and vintage sinks alike are at home in the country kitchen. Increasingly popular, antique sinks can be found at flea markets or purchased from salvage suppliers, then revamped to meet contemporary plumbing standards. Part of the magic of an old sink refitted for new use lies in its ability to evoke an earlier era — without

SINKS & *faucets*

the plumbing inconveniences of days gone by. A typical mid-19th-century sink, for example, had two pumps, one connected via cast-iron pipes to a well, the other linked to a rain cistern. Neither pump supplied hot water, however, and pipes often froze in winter, necessitating frequent trips to the outdoor well. Moreover, the sinks, made of wood, granite, or iron, required a daily scalding and occasional scouring with hot lye. Soapstone, widely used by the end of the 1800s, was a big improvement over these materials. The good looks of the soft stone, ranging from gray to green in color, were matched by the material's resistance to stains. These same qualities make old soapstone sinks (and reproductions, too) much in demand today.

Charmed by their old-fashioned looks, many homeowners opt to leave old sinks in place when remodeling a kitchen. Rather than discard a serviceable 1950s model, the owner of this remodeled kitchen set the original double basin — distinguished by broad shoulders with built-in drainage boards — on a new base (opposite). Black cabinets provide a dramatic contrast to the gleaming white enamel, suggesting the color scheme for the checked window valance.

The two most common materials used for making contemporary sinks are stainless steel and porcelain-enameled cast iron or steel. Light and easy to clean, stainless-steel sinks have either a nickel content (known as nickel-bearing) or a chrome content (non-nickel-bearing); nickel-bearing steel stays brighter longer and is more stain-resistant. Both types will last indefinitely and do not chip. Although the satin finish of a stainless-steel sink does tend to scratch with use, this results in an "heirloom" patina that many people find pleasing.

A porcelain-enameled finish is less durable than stainless steel and can chip, but is available in a variety of colors that can highlight — or even dictate — a kitchen's color scheme. Other, recently introduced options include resin-based solid surfacing material, which can merge seamlessly with a surrounding countertop made of the same finish, and resin-impregnated ceramic, also called quartz. These easy-care, chip-resistant materials come in textured and smooth finishes.

*With their homey look, sinks
made of soapstone (named for
its soft, soap-like feel) are a
popular choice for country kitchens.
The owner of a New Hampshire
house built from recycled materials
waited twenty years to use an
old soapstone sink he had salvaged;
set in a countertop cut from
a single piece of old timber, it
now holds a place of honor in
his new kitchen (opposite). The
soapstone sink in the kitchen
of a restored 1795 Cape was
custom-crafted to complement the
period interior (above).*

Most new sinks now come with one, two, or even three basins in
a variety of shapes and sizes geared to particular uses. Shallow basins are
good for working with food; deeper, wider basins are designed to
accommodate stockpots and roasting pans. A triple sink may have a
narrow center basin handy for rinsing utensils. Sinks can also be fitted
with a mechanical food disposal, which makes it convenient to peel
fruits and trim vegetables directly into the drain. (Before installing a
disposal, make sure such a device is permitted under your town
ordinances.) Other "extras" include cutting boards that fit atop a large
basin to convert the sink into a supplemental work surface.

Handsome faucets, many reproduced from 19th- and early-20th-
century models, also add period detail and character to a country
kitchen. In addition to classic chrome, hardware finishes include
resilient epoxy, available in dozens of colors, and epoxy-coated brass,
which requires no polishing. Hot-water and soap dispensers and
flexible spray nozzles are popular attachments.

New porcelain-enameled
sinks suit every purpose. A twin-
basin model (above) is designed
for both washing and rinsing
dishes. A cobalt-blue triple sink
(left) features a small central
basin, ideal for preparing fruits
and vegetables, and a food
disposal. The wide, flat faucet
handles can be worked with
an elbow when hands are full.
In a kitchen wet bar (opposite),
a small round stainless-steel
basin is fitted with a gooseneck
faucet that can accommodate
tall glasses and pitchers.

KITCHEN

collectibles

FROM WOODENWARE TO
DECORATED POTTERY, COUNTRY
COLLECTIBLES STILL HAVE AN
HONORED PLACE IN THE KITCHEN
TODAY. WITH THEIR SIMPLE
SHAPES AND BEAUTIFUL PATINAS,
SUCH TIME-WORN PIECES
CAN BE EASILY SHOWN OFF TO
ADVANTAGE IN CUPBOARDS,
ON SHELVES, OR HUNG FROM A
HAND-HEWN BEAM.

W O O D E N *w a r e*

The tradition of baking springerle cookies originated in the 1600s and came to this country with Germanic settlers. While molds were sold by professional woodcarvers, many were also homemade, often as presentation pieces to a sweetheart. Effectively displayed against a wood backdrop, springerle molds (opposite) depict 19th-century fashions, as well as fruits, flowers, and, of course, the heart. Rare burl bowls (above), some with handles shaped like ears, are the work of 18th-century Native Americans.

Among the earliest types of kitchenware used in the Colonies, wares made of treen (an old English dialect term for "wooden") served the American cook in the days before the Revolution, when most pottery had to be imported. The forests of the New World provided plenty of wood; carvers used hardwoods such as maple and birch for trenchers and mixing bowls, and softer pine for spoons and boxes. Scoops and bowls were also shaped out of burls — rounded growths on the trunks and branches of otherwise healthy trees. The beautiful grains of elm, ash, and maple burls were especially prized.

Favorite woodenware collectibles include the rectangular boxes that once held candles, pipes, and personal documents, as well as oval and round pantry boxes, covered buckets (sometimes called firkins), rolling pins, maple-sugar molds, and springerle boards, the decoratively carved molds used for making German cookies flavored with anise.

Because cleaning can be harmful, antique woodenware should not be used for serving food. With their simple designs and beautiful patinas, however, wooden collectibles stand on their own as display pieces, offering warmth and a sense of history.

Woodenware often reveals the craftsman's determination to make the utilitarian beautiful. Even pantry boxes and staved buckets crafted in the early 1800s were enlivened with colored paint (opposite top). Wooden rolling pins (the black-and-white painted example is from Texas) make an intriguing display in an antique dough box (opposite bottom); pins carved from a single piece of wood are the rarest. Dairy farmers used carved stamps (right) to identify the butter they sold at market with a personal trademark. The three-dimensional mold on the second shelf made a house-shaped block of butter complete with windows and doors.

R E D *w a r e*

Redware was often the only pottery available to American Colonists, who used it for everything from storing pickles to serving food. Slip decoration sometimes enlivened the utilitarian pottery; yellow squiggles, seen on a pair of trenchers, or plates, displayed in a Massachusetts dining room (opposite), were a common pattern. This 18th-century tavern setup includes an antique newspaper spool, next to the fruit. Jugs for fermented beverages, which required stoppers to retard evaporation, had narrow throats for easy sealing (above).

The first pottery produced by European settlers in America was probably redware, a simple, inexpensive type of earthenware fired to a red color and coated with a clear lead glaze. Made in the Colonies as early as 1650 by "pot bakers" who used a common brick clay heavily laced with iron oxide, redware trenchers, platters, jugs, crocks, and bowls were a kitchen staple for the next century and a half in frontier homes where imported goods were scarce. To give the humble pottery a festive appearance, designs in black or yellow slip (a mixture of clay and water blended to the consistency of cream) were dribbled or trailed onto the body of a piece before firing.

Porous and sensitive to extreme temperatures, redware broke easily and seldom saw service in more than one kitchen; pieces predating 1800 are rare indeed. In the 1830s, sturdier pottery such as graniteware and yellowware began replacing redware. However, some makers stayed in business until the 1880s, despite the fact (known as early as 1785) that the lead glaze was toxic. For this reason, collectors know never to use vintage redware to serve food; nonetheless, the pottery may be displayed with pride and admired it for its connection to the past.

With its simple shapes and graphic decoration, redware can easily be shown off to advantage; even a single piece makes an effective display. A slip-decorated redware charger, or platter, joins a set of early-19th-century miniature ironware implements (above), including a one-cup kettle on a broiler. Reproduction redware is now widely available; new and old pieces alike occupy a pine plate-drying rack (opposite).

The "Pine Kitchen" of Beauport (overleaf), a 1907 museum house in Gloucester, Massachusetts, features a fine collection of redware displayed in a corner cupboard and dish dresser. In addition to basic kitchen- and tablewares like these, roof tiles, pipes, and even toys were once fashioned from the inexpensive pottery.

Y E L L O W *w a r e*

Classic forms and soft colors give yellowware a surprisingly contemporary appearance, especially when pieces are featured in simple, uncluttered surroundings. In a sparsely decorated dining room (opposite), a pine hutch silhouettes the sculptural shapes of bowls and pitchers found in the Midwest. A trio of bowls (above) displays typical brown-and-white bands; the seaweed patterns were produced when a blue-colored glaze was allowed to run into the background color. The tortoise-shell pie plate is an example of Rockingham pottery.

Robust good looks, a sturdy constitution, and thoroughly practical nature have earned yellowware a place of honor in households everywhere. Perhaps more than any other collectible, this trusted earthenware embodies the unpretentious spirit of yesterday's country kitchens, where cooks relied on yellowware bowls for everything for making bread dough to mixing cake batter. They baked pies in yellowware pie plates, served tapioca in yellowware custard cups, and heated scalloped potatoes in covered yellowware casseroles.

Produced in quantity from about 1830 until the mid-1900s, primarily in factories in Staffordshire, England, and in East Liverpool, Ohio, yellowware was tougher than its predecessor, redware, owing to a protective glaze fired at high temperatures. Beneath the transparent glaze lay a coat of yellow, ranging in hue from palest buff to deep pumpkin (English yellowware was often lined in white). Pieces were typically decorated with simple bands of white or brown, or blue, green, or brown sponging. Embossed decoration, such as diamonds and scallop patterns, were also used.

Among the rarest and most coveted yellowware pieces collected

today are those manufactured before 1860 and marked by their maker, as well as wares sponged in green. Newer yellowware, however, is also appreciated. Collectors enjoy searching for different forms with the same decorative patterns, for example, or the challenge of putting together a set of bowls in graduated sizes.

Because yellowware was considered ovenproof, it was often used for casseroles, cake molds, and other kinds of bakeware, and these can still be found at auctions and flea markets. Look also for Rockingham, a type of yellowware decorated with a mottled brown glaze. Rockingham may be found in mugs, teapots, pitchers, and decorative display pieces, including animal figurines.

Because it saw heavy use, old yellowware is often stained. While vintage pieces can still be used for cooking and serving, they should never be bleached when washed, as this may break down the glazing and cause a piece to deteriorate.

An extensive collection of yellowware (above) includes a rare matching set of seven embossed mixing bowls with blue-glazed rims along with a variety of pudding and cake molds; the step-back cupboard displaying the sturdy earthenware dates to the 1850s. Among a group of 19th-century yellowware bowls tucked atop kitchen cupboards (opposite) are two examples with handy spouts for pouring batter into baking pans.

SPONGE*ware*

Searching for every known spongeware pattern and form could keep a collector busy for a lifetime. A Missouri homeowner has made a start, displaying pitchers, bowls, vases, crocks, and a rare teapot with lid intact in an antique cherry cupboard (opposite). Although spongeware was first produced in England around 1770, most pieces found in America today were made here in the 19th century. Common during this period, milk pitchers (above) moved stylishly from icebox to table. The green sponged decoration on the smaller pitcher is highly unusual.

Although it was mass-produced in tremendous numbers in America from about 1830 to 1940, spongeware often appears to be the work of individual craftsmen rather than the product of an assembly line. This is because the decoration itself was still applied by hand; the countless stylistic variations and subtle imperfections that resulted give the utilitarian ware a distinct warmth and personality.

It is the decoration, in fact, not the clay type, that defines spongeware, which includes any pottery (such as yellowware, stoneware, pearlware, and creamware) whose surface patterns have been dabbed on with a sponge or fabric swab, sometimes in conjunction with transfer patterns. Color combinations include the ubiquitous blue-on-white and rarer green-on-white, as well as tricolor layers of brown, green, and ocher. Unusual coloring adds value to a piece; examples marked with the maker's name (Ott & Brewer or International Potteries, for instance) and rarer forms such as teapots, large platters, and trivets are sought after. Casseroles and baking dishes are more common; moving with ease from oven to table, these continue to serve both cook and collector alike.

M O C H A *w a r e*

Now one of the most coveted antique pottery types, mochaware was made primarily for use in taverns. Tankards and smaller mugs join a saltshaker, eggcup, and creamer (opposite). The small mug on the first shelf from the top boasts a rare "scrambled" pattern that resembles marble. Assorted pieces (above), including pitchers and mugs, exhibit the characteristic exuberance of mochaware designs.

A distinctive decorated pottery made from the late 1700s until the 1850s, mochaware derives its name from its vivid and fanciful patterns rather than from the clay body (which might be one of several different types of earthenware, such as creamware, pearlware, or yellowware). Many of the designs, usually applied over a white or buff base color, recall the mottled markings of mochastone, a type of agate found near the Arabian port of Mocha.

Other striking patterns, however, also attract the interest of collectors, including looping earthworms (also called rope twists), cat's-eyes, polka dots, tortoiseshell, and wavy lines. Among the most beautiful are the delicate mosslike motifs that often resemble fan coral. These were created when a solution called mocha tea, a curious blend of tobacco juice, turpentine, and urine, was dripped onto a wet

background glaze, where it flowed into intricate designs. Usually, mochaware motifs were superimposed on broad solid-colored bands, most often in ocher, brown, blue, or green. As many as 26 bands in graduated sizes might festoon a single large piece, such as a jug.

Very little mochaware was produced in America, where pre-Revolutionary pub owners relied on English potters to supply them with mugs, bowls, and other necessities of tavern life. Pitchers and teapots were also prevalent; plates, however, were rare.

Mochaware is sometimes called banded creamware because most pieces made before 1830 had a creamware base; subsequently, several other types of clay body were also used. Some collectors seek out a single form of mochaware, such as shakers (left), while others create joyous displays by mixing shapes and patterns (opposite). Exhibiting mochaware inside a glass-front cabinet like this Minnesota pine cupboard is a good idea; pieces remain relatively dust-free and require less handling.

G R A N I T E *w a r e*

Displayed in quantity, graniteware makes a powerful statement in a homey country kitchen (opposite). While covered coffeepots like those arrayed above the stove are relatively common, the percolator and double boiler on the table are rare. Electric hot plates and children's wares (above) are also hard to find; the pewter-trimmed teapots and coffeepots date to the 19th century.

After generations of lugging, hoisting, and scrubbing cumbersome cast-iron pots and pans, homemakers in the late 19th century greeted graniteware with heartfelt gratitude. Introduced at the 1876 Centennial Exposition in Philadelphia, this revolutionary enamel-coated metal cookware (made first of sheet iron and later of steel) was lightweight as well as easy to clean. The new ware was pretty, too. By the end of World War I, dozens of manufacturers were offering it in every imaginable shade of blue, as well as in red, yellow, lavender, emerald, black, pink, and brown. Some pieces came in solid colors, while others boasted distinctive mottled, marble- and granite-like markings. During World War II, many cooks offered up their graniteware during scrap-metal drives, but thousands of pieces survive, due largely to the ware's remarkable durability.

A Tappan range with marbleized
doors shows off double boilers
and large coffeepots in a late-
19th-century turquoise pattern
(above left); on the floor is
a graniteware butter churn. Blue-
and-white pieces in a mottled
pattern include a large bucket,
oversized basins, and a covered pie
plate on the stove (above right).
A Hoosier cupboard (opposite)
shows off ladles, canisters,
and scales, along with a funnel,
grater, and muffin tin.

Graniteware was extremely
popular until the 1930s, when
aluminum cookware began to
replace it. As a rule of thumb,
the heavier a piece is, the
earlier its date. Collectors seek
examples stamped with the
manufacturer's name, including
the St. Louis Stamping Co.,
LaLance and Grosjean (L & G),
and Jacob Vollrath. Remarkably
durable, many pieces have
passed down through several
generations of the same family.

F L O W *b l u e*

While most flow-blue dinnerware was manufactured in England, it was exported in quantity and found its greatest popularity in America. Collectors covet individual pieces — ranging from teapots to tureens — as well as complete place settings for 12. This Wisconsin kitchen displays only a small portion of the 30 different patterns the owners have found. Prized pieces include the elegant covered cheese dish, dinner plates, and a converted oil lamp by the sink (opposite). A 1920 Magic Chef gas stove shows off a platter and serving dishes (above).

Of the many blue-and-white wares ever produced, flow blue (or flowing blue) is one of the most sought after and best loved today. Marketed primarily as inexpensive dinnerware, these lovely dishes were usually made with a delicate-looking semiporcelain (white ironstone) base, and thus had a slightly formal look that continues to contribute Victorian elegance to table settings and displays today.

The first examples of flow blue were actually produced by accident. Around 1820, an English potter mistakenly allowed a volatile substance like ammonia to mingle with the blue cobalt-oxide decoration before final glazing; during firing, the design "flowed," or bled, creating a blurred yet appealing effect. Soon English potters had perfected the technique and were exporting the new ware all over Europe and America. By 1850, more than 1,500 designs (most done with transfer patterns) were being made both here and abroad. At first Oriental themes dominated, but by the late Victorian era floral and scenic patterns held sway. Flow-blue production had all but ceased by the early years of the 20th century, but recommenced about 25 years ago because of popular demand.

The following resource listings for the kitchens profiled in Chapter Two refer to national manufacturers unless otherwise noted.

KITCHEN *resources*

TRADITIONAL

Design and craftsmanship:
THE WORKSHOPS
OF DAVID T. SMITH
Morrow, OH

SOUTH *western*

Design:
COUNTRY LIVING MAGAZINE
in collaboration with
ALESSANDRO DE GREGORI of
FORMICA CORPORATION

Cabinet surfaces, checkerboard and stainless backsplashes, counter and sink (Surrell solid surfacing): FORMICA

Cabinet hardware:
ARNOLD GOLDSTEIN
New York, NY

Cooktop, range hood, and wall ovens: THERMADOR

Door and hardware:
SOUTHWEST DOOR COMPANY
Tucson, AZ

Faucet: DELTA

Floor tiles: SUMMITVILLE

Refrigerator: AMANA

NEW *expressions*

Architecture:
STEPHEN R. KNUTSON
Knutson Designs, Evanston, IL

Backsplash, countertop, and tabletop (Surrell solid surfacing): FORMICA

Cabinetry: WOOD-MODE

Chandelier and sconce:
PERIOD LIGHTING FIXTURES
Chester, CT

Cooktop, dishwasher, microwave ovens, refrigerator, and wall oven: JENN-AIR

Counter, floor, and wall tiles:
AMERICAN OLEAN

Lattice Wall: AMERICAN
PLYWOOD ASSOCIATION
Tacoma, WA

Paint: PRATT & LAMBERT

Sinks and faucets: KOHLER

EUROPEAN *flair*

Design:
JENNIFER BRET FAGAN
BRET-PARKER INTERIORS
Norwalk, CT

Cabinetry: WOOD-MODE

Dishwasher: GENERAL ELECTRIC

Oven: CALORIC

Sink (blue ceramic): AMERICAN
STANDARD

Tiles: COUNTRY FLOORS
New York, NY

N O S T A L G I A *t i m e*

Cabinetry: MERILLAT

Cooktop, dishwasher, and
ovens: WHIRLPOOL

Countertop: FORMICA

Faucet, handles, and sink:
AMERICAN STANDARD

Floor tiles: ARMSTRONG

U R B A N *a f f a i r*

Design:
GREGORY A. ROACH
GAR ASSOCIATES
with KERRY FIDLER
New York, NY

Cabinets: LES CARE

Cabinet surfaces and countertop
(Surell solid surfacing): FORMICA

Chandelier: IRONWARE
INTERNATIONAL
Nashville, TN

Dishwasher: KITCHEN AID

Faucet: CHICAGO FAUCET

Floor tiles: HASTINGS TILE
New York, NY

Mountain stone veneer:
ELDORADO STONE
Carnation, WA

Refrigerator: EUROFLAIR
(a division of Frigidaire)

Sink: VERMONT SOAPSTONE
Perkinsville, VT

S I M P L Y *s h a k e r*

Design:
COUNTRY LIVING MAGAZINE
in collaboration with
TIMOTHY J. ADEN, CKD
SAWHILL CUSTOM
KITCHENS AND DESIGNS
Minneapolis, MN

Cabinets and woodwork:
PLATO WOODWORK
Plato, MN

Chairs, baskets, and Shaker accessories:
SHAKER WORKSHOPS
Concord, MA

Countertop (Gibraltar solid
surfacing): WILSONART

Dishwasher, wall ovens, and
refrigerator: KITCHEN AID

Faucets and sink: KOHLER

Flooring: HARRIS-TARKETT

Paint: MARTIN-SENOUR

Pot Rack: STUDIO STEEL
New Preston, CT

Tile: DAL-TILE

The following organizations
can provide information about
kitchen products and professional
design services.

AMERICAN INSTITUTE OF
ARCHITECTS
1735 New York Avenue, N.W.
Washington, D.C. 20006

ANTIQUE STOVE ASSOCIATION
219-583-6465

NATIONAL ASSOCIATION OF THE
REMODELING INDUSTRY
9667-B Main Street
Fairfax, VA 22031

NATIONAL KITCHEN AND BATH
ASSOCIATION
687 Willow Grove Street
Hackettstown, NJ 07840

NATIONAL PAINT AND COATINGS
ASSOCIATION
1500 Rhode Island Avenue, N.W.
Washington, D.C. 20005

NATIONAL TRUST FOR HISTORIC
PRESERVATION
1785 Massachusetts Avenue, N.W.
Washington, D.C. 20036

NATIONAL WOOD FLOORING
ASSOCIATION
233 Old Meramec Station Road
Manchester, MO 63021

2, 4, 6   Jessie Walker

8   Keith Scott Morton

10-11   Jessie Walker

14, 15   Allan Baillie and Debra De Boise

16-17, 18-19, 19, 20, 20-21
    Keith Scott Morton

22   Lilo Raymond

23, 24-25, 26, 27 (left and right)
    Keith Scott Morton

28-29, 30, 31   Jessie Walker

32 (top and bottom)   Keith Scott Morton

122   Jessie Walker

123, 124   Keith Scott Morton

125 (top and bottom), 126   Feliciano

127   Michael Dunne

128   Keith Scott Morton

129 (top) Keith Scott Morton;
    (bottom) Gus Francisco and
    Allan Baillie

132   Keith Scott Morton

134 (top left and right) Keith Scott Morton;
    (bottom left and right) Jessie Walker

PHOTOGRAPHY*credits*

33 (top and bottom) Feliciano

34   Keith Scott Morton

35, 36   Jessie Walker

37 (top) Keith Scott Morton;
    (bottom) John Vaughan

38-39, 39, 40-41, 43, 42-43
    Keith Scott Morton

46, 48, 49   Jessie Walker

50, 53-53, 54, 55 (top and bottom)
    Keith Scott Morton

56, 57, 58, 59, 60, 61   Jessie Walker

64-65, 66, 67 (left and right)   Kari Haavisto

68, 70-71, 72, 73   Jeremy Samuelson

74, 76-77, 78 (top left and right, bottom),
    79, 80, 82-83, 84 (top and bottom),
    85, 88, 90, 91, 92, 93, 94
    Keith Scott Morton

95 (top left) Joshua Greene;
    (top right) Jessie Walker;
    (bottom left and right)
    Keith Scott Morton

96-97   Keith Scott Morton

98   Jessie Walker

99 (top) Paul Kopelow;
    (bottom) Keith Scott Morton

100   Paul Kopelow

102   Keith Scott Morton

103 (top) Jessie Walker;
    (bottom) Jeremy Samuelson

104-105, 106, 107, 108-109
    Keith Scott Morton

110   Jessie Walker

111 (top, bottom right) Keith Scott Morton;
    (bottom left) Ben Rosenthal

113, 114, 116 (top and bottom)
    Keith Scott Morton

117   Pizzi/Thompson

118   Doug Kennedy

119, 120 (top and bottom),
    121   Keith Scott Morton

135, 136, 137 (left and right),
    138, 139 (top and bottom),
    140, 141 Keith Scott Morton

142   Jessie Walker

144   Paul Kopelow

145 (top) Keith Scott Morton;
    (bottom) Peter Margonelli

146   Jessie Walker

148 (top) Jessie Walker;
    (bottom) Jeremy Samuelson

149   Pizzi/Thompson

150-151, 152, 153, 154, 156
    Keith Scott Morton

157   Allan Baillie and Debra De Boise

158 (top) Jessie Walker;
    (bottom) Keith Scott Morton

159   Keith Scott Morton

162   Jessie Walker

163, 164 (top and bottom) Tom Yee

165   Jessie Walker

166, 167   Keith Scott Morton

168   Tom Yee

169, 170-171   Keith Scott Morton

172   John Vaughan

173, 174   Keith Scott Morton

175   Peter Margonelli

176   Jessie Walker

177, 178   Paul Kopelow

179   Keith Scott Morton

180   Paul Kopelow

181   Keith Scott Morton

182, 183 Steven Mays

184 (left) Steven Mays;
    (right) Paul Kopelow

185   Steven Mays

186, 187   Jessie Walker

190, 192   Keith Scott Morton